Killer Disasters

FLOODS AND TSUNAMIS

DOREEN GONZALES

PowerKiDS press.

New York

Published in 2013 by The Rosen Publishing Group, Inc.
29 East 21st Street, New York, NY 10010

First Edition

Editor: Amelie von Zumbusch
Book Design: Greg Tucker

Photo Credits: Cover Robert Nickelsberg/Stringer/Getty Images; p. 4 Caitlin Mirra/Shutterstock.com; pp. 5, 12–13 A. S. Zain/Shutterstock.com; p. 6 Skynavin/Shutterstock.com; p. 7 (top) Bloomberg/Getty Images; p. 7 (bottom) AFP/Stringer/Getty Images; p. 8 Mark Sayer/Shutterstock.com; p. 9 (top) David Davis/Shutterstock.com; p. 9 (bottom) Mike Buchheit/Shutterstock.com; p. 10 Wil Tilroe-Otte/Shutterstock.com; p. 11 Scott Barbour/Getty Images News/Getty Images; p. 13 (bottom) AFP/Stringer/Getty Images; p. 14–15 Jon Sheer/Flickr/Getty Images; p. 16 Xidong Luo/Shutterstock.com; p. 17 (top) Daniel Taeger/Shutterstock.com; p. 17 (bottom) Roberto Tetsuo Okamura/Shutterstock.com; p. 18 H. Armstong Roberts/Retrofile/Getty Images; p. 19 Jeffrey M. Frank/Shutterstock.com; p. 20 Nigel Treblin/DDP/Getty Images; p. 21 Timothy A. Clary/AFP/Getty Images; p. 22 Bernhard Richter/Shutterstock.com.

Library of Congress Cataloging-in-Publication Data

Gonzales, Doreen.
 Floods and tsunamis / by Doreen Gonzales. — 1st ed.
   p. cm. — (Killer disasters)
 Includes index.
 ISBN 978-1-4488-7438-5 (library binding) — ISBN 978-1-4488-7511-5 (pbk.) —
 ISBN 978-1-4488-7585-6 (6-pack)
 1. Floods—Juvenile literature. 2. Tsunamis—Juvenile literature. I. Title.
 GB1399.G66 2013
 363.34'93—dc23
                                  2011044896

Manufactured in the United States of America

CPSIA Compliance Information: Batch #B3S12PK: For Further Information contact Rosen Publishing, New York, New York at 1-800-237-9932

CONTENTS

OUT OF CONTROL!

All living things need water. This water comes from rain and snow. It is found in rivers and lakes, too. Sometimes, the amount of water gets out of control and a flood happens. Rivers and lakes become so full that water spills over their banks. When **dams** give way, the water they hold back pours out. Floods are not always harmful. However, some ruin buildings and kill animals. Floods can even kill people.

Floods often cover roads. This can leave people with no way to get out of areas where the water is still rising.

In 2004, a major tsunami swept this boat onto land in Aceh, Indonesia.

Ocean water can also become wild. Huge waves called tsunamis wash across beaches onto the land beyond. They sweep away people and buildings. **Landslides**, volcanoes, and undersea earthquakes can all cause tsunamis.

WATER, WATER EVERYWHERE

Many things cause floods. Water from rain flows into rivers and lakes. Long or hard rains sometimes fill these bodies of water. Once they are full, if more rain falls, it has nowhere to go. It runs onto nearby land.

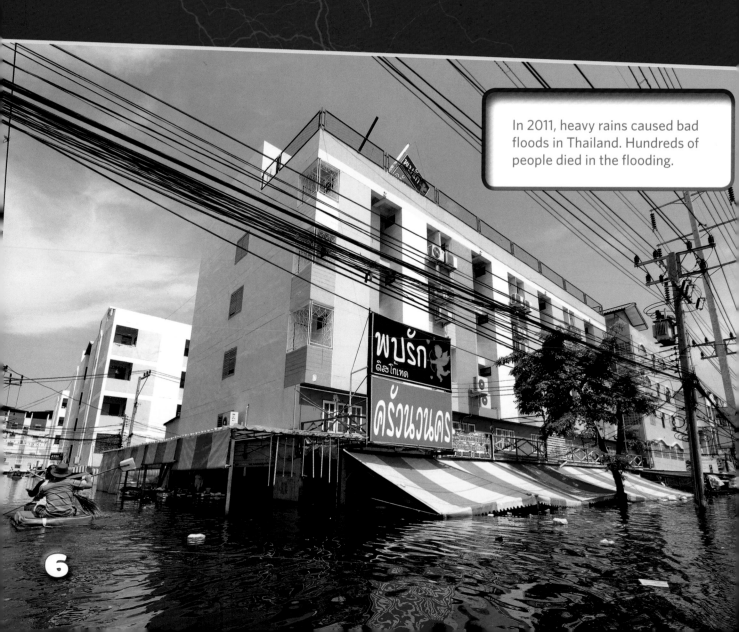

In 2011, heavy rains caused bad floods in Thailand. Hundreds of people died in the flooding.

Melting snow can also cause flooding. Melted snow flows to rivers and lakes. If snow melts too quickly, they can flood. This often happens when a lot of snow is followed by several days of warm weather.

Storms called **hurricanes** can cause flooding, too. Many bring heavy rains. Their strong winds can push water from oceans or lakes onto land, too.

IN A FLASH!

Flash floods are floods that happen suddenly. Flash floods are common at the bottoms of mountains and hills after heavy rains. Water runs quickly down these slopes and pools at the bottom. Many flash floods happen in **canyons** and other places where rain is funneled into narrow areas.

Some places where flash floods are common have signs that warn people, such as this one.

POTENTIAL FLASH FLOOD AREAS

NEXT 6 MILES

Top: Flash floods helped shape South Antelope Canyon. The canyon is on Navajo lands in Arizona. Flash floods are still a danger there. *Bottom*: This flash flood happened in Grand Canyon National Park, in Arizona.

Heavy desert rains can also create flash floods. Desert soils cannot take in much water. Rainstorms in cities can cause flash flooding in places like underground parking garages.

When a dam breaks, it can also cause a flash flood. Water rushing over a broken dam can pour into the area below quite suddenly.

FLOODS FROM THE OCEAN

Storm surges cause coastal floods. A storm surge happens when winds from hurricanes or other storms push water onto the shoreline. Strong hurricanes can make storm surges over 25 feet (8 m) high.

Storm surges cause the sea level to rise, as you can see in this photograph.

The tsunami that hit the Indian Ocean in 2004 left more than one and a half million kids homeless.

Tsunamis can cause costal floods, too. Tsunamis strike coasts with little warning. Some are not very high at all. Others can be 100 feet (30 m) tall. Tsunamis can move up to 600 miles per hour (965 km/h).

In 2004, an earthquake rocked the floor of the Indian Ocean near Indonesia. It set off one of the worst tsunamis in history. Within an hour, waves hit seacoasts all around that ocean.

Disaster in the Indian Ocean!

Date:	**December 26, 2004**
Magnitude of the earthquake that caused the tsunami:	**9.0**
Number of atomic bombs that would make the same amount of energy as the earthquake:	**23,000**
Height of highest tsunami waves:	**15 feet (5 m)**

Distance the tsunami traveled:	**3,000 miles (5,000 km)**
Number of countries hit:	**11**
Number of people listed as dead:	**169,752**
Number of people listed as missing:	**127,294**

Tsunami waves hitting Koh Raya, Thailand.

TSUNAMI IN JAPAN

In 2010, an earthquake that shook the seafloor off Japan created a powerful tsunami. Its waves reached 30 feet (9 m). Ocean water rushed across Japanese beaches and through cities. It carried away cars, buildings, and people. Dams burst and power lines were knocked over.

Quickly flowing water destroyed parts of nearby **nuclear** power plants. **Radiation**, a form of energy that can make people sick, leaked from them. It will be many years before scientists know how many people were made sick by the radiation.

The tsunami itself left almost 20,000 people dead or missing. Thousands more were left without homes.

This fishing boat was washed ashore by the tsunami that hit Japan in 2010.

AGAIN AND AGAIN

Some areas have had many floods. The Yellow River, in China, has flooded for centuries, killing millions of people. The river's waters are full of **silt**. This fine dirt falls to the river bottom, building its bed higher and higher. Water flows from the high parts onto nearby land. Today, dams and high banks called **dikes** control the flooding.

The Yellow River is also called the Huang He. It is the second-longest river in China.

The Netherlands has also had many floods. Much of this country lies below sea level. People there once built dikes to hold the ocean back. These dikes often gave way and caused deadly flooding. Today, strong dams keep the Netherlands dry.

Hundreds of years ago, people in the Netherlands started building windmills, such as the ones below, to control floods. More recently, they have built dams, such as the ones shown above.

THE JOHNSTOWN FLOOD

One of the worst floods in the United States happened in Johnstown, Pennsylvania, in 1889. Johnstown sits in a valley of the Allegheny Mountains.

That year, a spring thunderstorm filled a lake above the town. The water pushed against a dam and made it weak. Then

This is one of the 1,600 homes that were destroyed in the Johnstown Flood.

P.R.R.

The dam that broke and caused the Johnstown Flood was the South Fork Dam. It sat on the South Fork Little Conemaugh River, seen here.

the dam burst. Water poured out of the lake and down the mountainside. Within an hour, a wall of water was rushing into Johnstown.

The water swept through the town, taking people and buildings with it. The flood killed more than 2,000 people.

WATCHING FOR WATER

One way that scientists study floods is by building **computer models** of past floods. This helps them predict how future floods might behave. The National Weather Service closely watches rivers that might flood. It sends out warnings to officials and news stations where flooding might occur.

Scientists at tsunami warning centers watch for undersea earthquakes using instruments called **seismographs**. When an undersea earthquake happens, they look

This scientist is studying an earthquake that happened off the coast of Samoa and caused a tsunami in 2009.

Scientists' warnings give people time to evacuate, or leave for safety, before a disaster hits.

for signs that a tsunami is forming. They use information sent to them by special **sensors** in the ocean. They can also track tsunamis with **satellites** in space. As soon as possible, they send warnings to the places where tsunamis could hit.

Keep Safe!

Too much water can be deadly. During a flood, never walk through water that is deeper than your feet. Stay away from ditches and storm drains. Move to higher ground.

Listen for tsunami warnings when you are near the coast. An unusual rise or fall in ocean waters can be a sign that a tsunami is coming. If this happens, move away from the beach. Knowing what to do can keep you safe in a disaster!

TSUNAMI EVACUATION ROUTE

Some places where tsunamis are known to be a danger have signs that people can follow to reach safety.

GLOSSARY

CANYONS (KAN-yunz) Deep, narrow valleys.

COMPUTER MODELS (kum-PYOO-ter MAH-dulz) Computer programs that show what might happen in real life.

DAMS (DAMZ) Large walls built in rivers that control when water can pass.

DIKES (DYKS) Tall walls that are built to hold back water.

HURRICANES (HUR-ih-kaynz) Storms with strong winds and heavy rain.

LANDSLIDES (LAND-slydz) Movements of rock or earth down a slope.

NUCLEAR (NOO-klee-ur) Having to do with the power created by splitting atoms, the smallest bits of matter.

RADIATION (ray-dee-AY-shun) Rays of light, heat, or energy that spread outward from something.

SATELLITES (SA-tih-lyts) Spacecraft that circle Earth.

SEISMOGRAPHS (SYZ-muh-grafs) Tool that measure movement in Earth's crust.

SENSORS (SEN-sorz) Tools that pick up facts.

SILT (SILT) Fine bits of earth, smaller than sand grains, found at the bottoms of lakes and streams.

INDEX

WEBSITES

Due to the changing nature of Internet links, PowerKids Press has developed an online list of websites related to the subject of this book. This site is updated regularly. Please use this link to access the list: www.powerkidslinks.com/kd/flood/